THE SILENT CRIES OF

A Black Girl

SUPPORTING GIRLS WHO HAVE
BEEN SEXUALLY ABUSED

THE SILENT CRIES OF

A Black Girl

SUPPORTING GIRLS WHO HAVE BEEN SEXUALLY ABUSED

by:

SIAH B. HAGIN

VINE
PUBLISHING

Vine Publishing's name and logo are trademarks of Vine Publishing, Inc.

ISBN: 979-8-9867471-0-1 (paperback)
ISBN: 978-0-578-94534-7 (e-book)

Library of Congress Cataloging-in-Publication Data
Library of Congress Control Number: 2022915992

Published by Vine Publishing, Inc.
New York, NY
www.vinepublish.com

Printed in the United States of America

DEDICATION

This book is dedicated to every young girl who is living with the aftermath of sexual abuse and to the adults who create safe spaces for them to speak their truth.

TABLE OF CONTENTS

INTRODUCTION

The uprising of the #MeToo Movement, and other ally organizations that have come together to take a stand against abuse, has forced a conversation. The conversation about protecting/supporting our girls is a necessary measure. The fall of many prominent celebrities of all races and cultural backgrounds sends a message that "enough is enough", and survivors will no longer be silent. There is a powerful movement that is sweeping across this country. The message is one that is loud and clear: Stand up and Be Heard. The atmosphere has been set and the time is now. Therefore, now is the perfect time to have this conversation.

Abuse thrives in the darkness. It is free to roam through every part of your life, just as one roams through the corridors of a building, destroying everything in its path – joy, peace, love. It comes in like a thief, but then it settles in. It takes up permanent residence, each day more comfortable than the day before. After some time has passed, it is no longer an intruder, but a friend you tolerate. You know that friend you really don't like but you put up with? That friend you can hang with sometimes, but can't be bothered to see at other times. That's what happens when we allow abuse to stay too long. Abuse loves the darkness. It steals your peace until you can no longer recognize that it was once the enemy of your soul. It haunts you through every friendship and relationship until you realize its presence is unwanted, and detrimental to your physical and mental health.

The pain a young girl has when she has been subjected to abuse is unbearable. She is no longer herself. She cannot function like she once did. She is robbed of her youth and is bound by a trauma that haunts her. The sweet, innocent girl who saw life through a rose-colored lens is gone. She is forced to grow up too soon, in bondage, not understanding how to be free.

This book is a guide and a tool to help parents learn to recognize the signs of abuse and provide steps to support your daughter through this difficult process. This book should be read by parents, caregivers, youth counselors, aunties, grandparents, etc. If you play a significant role in the life of a pre-adolescent or adolescent girl, this is a book you need. The language will primarily be directed to parents, with a focus on the African American community. I will use the terms "book" and "guide" interchangeably throughout. In it, I share my story to give that young girl who has not found her voice the courage to speak her truth, and to help struggling loved ones who may recognize signs of sexual abuse but may be too afraid to act. This book is for you.

This is a story of transparency and vulnerability in the face of abuse. This is the way I must share my journey to healing with you. Through my transparency and vulnerability, my prayer is that at least one young girl can be saved. Perhaps one girl will have a moment of bravery to share what she has been subjected to. As I share, please know that I relive each painful moment; however, it's my choice. I choose to tell this story and relive the moments because I have survived it all. I have been healed and delivered. Abuse no longer has control over me. I choose to relive it in order to aid in someone else's healing, and that makes all the difference in the world.

THE SURVIVOR

CHAPTER 1

The Innocence of a Young Girl

My home was one with a strong foundation of morals and standards. Two loving parents that provided everything my brother and I needed. I was a happy child, and my parents raised me to love myself and to love God. My father made sure I carried myself like a young lady. I was his "little girl". Like most fathers, his job was to make sure that no harm came to me and that I remained a little girl for as long as possible. He was my protector, and he taught my brother to be my protector when I was not in his presence.

My upbringing was based on traditional, conventional thinking, or perhaps old-school thinking that stemmed from my parents' southern roots. My mother taught me how to conduct myself as a "young lady"—how to care for a home, along with other responsibilities. There was a clear line of distinction between my brother and me. He was a boy, and I was a girl. He had to learn how to mow the lawn, rake the leaves, take the garbage out, and fix things around the home. I was not exposed to too much too soon. There were rules and boundaries that my parents had for us to ensure that we could take care of ourselves and make our own way in this "harsh world". School was of the utmost importance. I was taught, through education, that I could be anything I could imagine. "Take advantage of every opportunity," my parents would say. "Opportunities open doors." After all, my success was my parents' success because I represented them in everything I did. With this in mind, I made sure never to do anything to embarrass them or myself.

There were rules and high expectations. I was expected to succeed because I had the capability. I was given the tools to do so, and I could go far. I was a happy young girl who was loved and protected. A perfect environment for a young girl to thrive, until the visitor.

THE VISITOR

It was not until my early pre-teens that my life took a dramatic turn. The presence of a visitor changed everything. A relative came to live with us. The plan was that he would stay with us until he was able to make his own way. He had recently relocated and wanted to make a life for himself in New York. He needed a place he could stay until he could be independent, and our doors were opened.

This was a well-known tradition within our family, and something my parents knew very well. Their migration from the south to the north was a hard road. They relied on the support of loved ones, which included staying with family up north until they were able to stand on their own. I recalled stories my parents told my brother and me as teens. These stories were shared as a reminder of the harsh world that awaited us. So, with this tradition in mind, my parents welcomed my cousin into our home. Naturally, I also welcomed him into our home and made him feel comfortable. I thought it was cool that one of my cousins would be staying with us for a while. It was like having another big brother I could talk to and bother. When my brother was not there to talk, I talked to my cousin. I was comfortable around him, and because I didn't always have to talk to my brother, it was a welcome change.

One method that abusers use to gain the trust of their victims is called "grooming". I will talk about this more later in the book, but let me say that my cousin was great at grooming. He knew what to say to make me comfortable, and he used it for his gain. My comfortability opened the door for abuse. My cousin took advantage of the situation and began touching me in inappropriate places. Like many acts of abuse, it starts subtle with a stroking of the shoulders and an accidental brush across the breast. The subtlety becomes more aggressive, and then you are completely and totally violated.

On multiple occasions, he sexually abused me, with each moment stripping away my innocence, and taking away what was sacred. It was not only sexual abuse but mental abuse as well. Everything that I knew to be certain shifted me into a place of obscurity. I questioned everything that I was taught. I was left confused and afraid. I was unsure of who I was or who I was to become. I thought, "Who is this person?" "Why is he doing this to me?" "What did I do to him to deserve this?" These questions boggled my mind, and I was constantly searching for answers.

In the face of continued sexual abuse, I retreated within myself and withdrew from the world around me. Every act of abuse left me hugging myself and rocking back and forth. I was trying to make sense of what had just happened and would continue to happen. Once a happy—albeit quiet and timid—child, I now lived in silent fear. I was afraid of him and the threats that spewed from his mouth—threats of future abuse. But, I was more afraid of what kind of woman I would become if the abuse continued. I saw myself as a teenage mother carrying a baby that was created from a place of pain and shame. Who would believe that I was raped?! The thought of a pain-filled future and the fear of what could happen, scared me enough to speak my truth.

THE DAY I FOUND MY VOICE

One particular day, I was on my way home from school but couldn't bring myself to go home, as I lived in fear of being home alone with my cousin. This was my life now. I was afraid to go home, but I was even more terrified of an unwanted teenage pregnancy, and that fear gave me the strength to open up to tell someone. "I have to tell my mom…I need to tell my mom… say something, Siah!" That evening, I attempted to muster the words to tell my mother, but I couldn't verbalize it. It was too hard. I knew I had to get it out, but how? How could I tell her that her baby girl was being abused? How could I tell her about all the violations – the pain and the shame? "Think, Siah! How are you going to say it?" My heart was beating fast, and I felt nervous. I wasn't sure how to tell her, but I knew this was an urgent matter and it demanded her immediate attention. So, after much thought, I decided to leave a note under her makeup compact, knowing she would find it there. That note was my attempt to save myself. Upon returning to my room, I waited anxiously for her to see the note. This was an opportune time. My cousin was not home, and I could speak to my parents freely. So, I waited, and after what felt like hours, she found the note and shared it with my father, who became enraged. "They know!" Immediately, relief washed over my soul because I had finally shared this horrible secret.

My father, the protector, could not fathom how he was unable to prevent something so horrible from happening to his daughter. He was devastated, and my mother was in great distress. As I think back on that night, I remember my mother's screams, my father's fists flying, and my abuser denying everything that had happened. Finally, I heard police sirens, and then there was a strange, eerie silence. The kind of silence when no one knows what to say. That silence stayed with me.

MY POWER

The abuse stopped when my cousin left the house; however, I was left to deal with a rollercoaster of emotions that haunted me for many years. My transition from my teen years to early adulthood was paved with anger, hurt, relief, fear, and a host of other emotions. I had been free from the weight of the abuse, but there were aftereffects. Fear still held me in bondage. I was afraid of running into my cousin. "If you see him, Siah, what are you going to say? What are you going to do?" These were constant thoughts. I wondered how I would respond when I saw him. Would I be confrontational, or would I flee or freeze? I would frequently rehearse my reaction to that scenario. I had also developed a distrust of people. While I mistrusted men the most, the betrayal I experienced developed into a generalized mistrust, and so I viewed most people as untrustworthy.

Year after year passed, and I struggled to put the pieces of my life back together again. I struggled with fear. I struggled with trust, love, and being loved. However, after years of feeling unworthy, damaged, and shameful, I arrived at a place of acceptance and peace. I accepted that while the abuse was a part of my life, it would not dictate my life or have power over my future. I understood that it was my abuser's desire to make me feel damaged and powerless; however, even in my broken state, I felt a drive within me to not let that happen.

The journey from damaged girl to healed woman has taught

me to love and believe in myself, but more importantly, to trust the God in me. I learned to trust the God that has healed and set me free. As a result, I have found my voice and I use my voice to help others. I am a survivor and an advocate. I no longer see my abuse as a curse, or a punishment. I haven't fully arrived, because truth be told, there are days when I still find it hard to believe that I am worthy to be loved, but those are the days when I lean on God the most. In those times, I remind myself that I am God's daughter, and I am loved. Those days also remind me that my voice is a powerful weapon.

(HER) VOICE IS A WEAPON

This is what every girl wants when they take that courageous step to disclose their trauma. They want to be heard and believed. They want to be vindicated and validated. They want to know that their voice matters. The voice of the survivor is powerful. *Her* voice—your daughter, niece, cousin, sister, friend—is a powerful weapon.

Recent changes in our society have proven that speaking our truth can be liberating. Our voices have collectively forced change in laws and policies to protect survivors. A survivor uses their voice to speak truth to power, and the most courageous act a survivor can do is share their story.

The first time a survivor shares their story is a transforming moment and part of the first step toward healing. It's the first step in being free—free from the darkness that abuse forces us to live in. Once we speak our truth, the abuse is exposed to light, and healing is possible. This happened when I decided to share my abuse with my parents. The day I shared my secret, I was believed by those who cared the most for me—my parents. That was a major step toward healing. We cannot heal from what we do not expose. As long as we stay in silence, we will continue to suffer in darkness. This is what makes our voice so powerful. It is

a matter of life and death.

UNDERSTANDING SEXUAL ABUSE

CHAPTER 2

What Is Sexual Abuse?

There are many misconceptions surrounding sexual abuse. However, let me start off by saying abuse is never the victim's fault. It is about power and control. The perpetrator uses their power to manipulate and control their victim. The perpetrator is often someone in an authoritative position. Sexual abuse can occur with a person of the same age; however, statistics have shown that it's rare.

Sexual abuse is forced behavior or against a person's will. It is unwanted and "unwelcomed". Sexual abuse includes unwanted touching, stroking, kissing, forced or manipulated sexual acts, as well as forced viewing of sexual acts. While you may have heard many versions of what sexual abuse is and is not, this is a definition to keep in mind.

Sexual abuse does not require penetration for it to be named "sexual abuse." Sexual abuse can happen to anyone and by anyone. This includes family members, friends, strangers, etc. However, it is important to note that most girls are familiar with their abuser.

GROOMING

Abusers often build a rapport with their victims by way of grooming. Grooming is a manipulative method used by abusers to build rapport with individuals they intend to sexually violate. The intention is to make their victims comfortable in their presence. Groomers use their relationship with their victims to lure them. The grooming process can be as short as several weeks, or as long as several years. It is intentional and calculated. The abuser is likely the last person you would suspect in your circle—that person your family knows well and regards with the least skepticism. The abuser may hold a high position or most likely respected in the community. He or she uses this to their advantage. While they may not threaten their victims, they will convince them that they will not be believed if they report the abuse. As a reminder, one of the biggest fears of victims is not being believed. The groomer knows this and uses this to keep their victims in control.

My abuser had the advantage of a family connection. He became that cool cousin I could hang with and talk to. At the age of fourteen (the age I was abused), having a cool cousin made life exciting and fun. The emotional connection established a comfortable environment for me and a path of least resistance for him to carry out his plan. To understand how abusers operate, in the following section I provide some statistics that elucidate their tactics, and how girls are grossly impacted by their abuse.

STATISTICS

While both boys and girls experience sexual abuse, statistics reveal that girls are significantly more victimized than boys. The stats below not only provide further insight, but also confirm the previous information provided about "Grooming." As shared, my abuser was a relative—someone who created a bond with me. Statistics reveal that victims are familiar with their abuser, which allows the abuser easy access to them.

The following statistics are from RAINN (Rape, Abuse & Incest National Network), the largest anti-violence organization:

- One in nine girls and one in fifty-three boys under the age of 18 experience sexual abuse or assault at the hands of an adult.

- Females ages 16-19 are 4 times more likely than the general population to be victims of rape, attempted rape, or sexual assault.

- 82 % of all victims under 18 are female.

- 93% are known by their perpetrator.

- 59% are acquaintances.

- 34% are family members and 7 % are strangers.

(RAINN, "Children and Teens: Statistics")

Now, while there is not a great deal of statistics on child sexual abuse and the African American community, I want to share a few statistics about sexual violence against black girls from The National Center on Violence against Women in the Black Community.

- One in four black girls will be sexually abused before the age of 18. (Remember, according to the RAINN stats, 1 in 9 girls will experience sexual abuse, therefore based research by the National Center on Violence against Women in the Black Community, we can surmise that African American girls are at higher risk of sexual abuse

- Among students, 11% of black girls in a national high school sample reported having been raped.

- African American girls and women, 12 years and older, experienced higher rates of rape and sexual assault than White, Asian, and Latina girls and women from 2005-2010. (The National Center on Violence against Women in the Black Community, 2018)

Lastly, while these statistics are staggering and are evidence of the impact of child sexual abuse, we must not forget that racism and mistrust within the African American community are barriers to reporting sexual abuse. As a result, many incidents of sexual abuse go unreported and abusers are free to abuse others.

BEHAVIOR AND POSSIBLE SIGNS

I was a quiet, shy girl. I stayed to myself and had few friends; that was just my personality. I was sheltered as a young girl and was not exposed to life experiences until I was older. I displayed no extreme behaviors, and therefore my parents were unable to detect that something was going on. At that age, I knew how to hide my symptoms out of fear of further abuse. Your child may attempt to do the same, especially if she is being threatened. She may not be able to put into words what she is feeling and instead begin to act out of character.

There are several possible signs and behavioral changes that may be present as a result of sexual abuse, and more than likely you have begun to see those changes in your daughter, niece, granddaughter, mentee, or some young lady around you. You may be thinking, "Something is not right!" Something has raised thoughts of concern and brought you to this place. I understand your concerns. Knowing your child's typical behavior will help you detect when something is wrong. This requires you to pay extra attention and keep an open line of communication with her, her friends, and extended family members.

I have provided answers below to some questions you may have. It is important to note that not all signs are experienced by individuals who have experienced abuse; however, these are some common signs.

POSSIBLE SIGNS:

- Nightmares or other sleeping problems without an explanation

- Seems distracted or distant

- Has a sudden change in eating habits

- Sudden mood swings: rage, fear, insecurity, or withdrawal

- Writes, draws, plays, or dreams of sexual or frightening images

- Develops new or unusual fear of certain people or places

- Refuses to talk about a secret shared with an adult or older child

- Exhibits adult-like sexual behaviors, language, and knowledge

- Isolation from peers, family and love ones

- Disinterest in things they once enjoyed

- Anxiety

- Chronic stomach pain and headaches

• Depression

TALKING TO YOUR DAUGHTER ABOUT THE ABUSE

You have noticed some signs and some changes in your daughter, and now it's time to have a conversation…but how do you approach the topic? Well, as a parent, you are going to rely on the rapport that you have built with your child when choosing to have this conversation. Hopefully, this is not the first time talking with them about "good touch versus bad touch" or "inappropriate touching". I am sure that, like most parents, you have told your child that if anyone touches them inappropriately, they should let you know. While this is a conversation that parents tend to have with their children, it is usually a one-time conversation, and so broaching the topic will require creating a safe, comforting space for your daughter to open up and speak.

When starting a sensitive conversation, your tone is just as important as what you say. A calm tone paired with a calm demeanor will yield better results than an angry or hostile one. Although you may be anxious or angry (particularly if you know the abuser), the focus is to get enough information to get the appropriate help for your child. Your tone and language should communicate care and concern. This will determine how comfortable your child will be during the talk and how much she shares. If, prior to talking with her, you feel like speaking to someone within your circle of support, please do so. Practice and review what you will say to ensure that it is communicated with love. This is a good time to remind you that your daughter's biggest fear is not being believed. As a parent, you may not understand everything, and I am sure you will have many questions, but trust that your questions will be answered in time. Talking with your daughter is a time to actively listen, affirm, and believe.

SEEKING SUPPORT AND THE AFRICAN AMERICAN COMMUNITY

CHAPTER 3

The African American Culture

The African American community has a problem. Yes, we do! The problem is rooted in our rich heritage. While our cultural norms have seen us through the most challenging and grueling times in our history, there are some that have become problematic for us as a people. One of these norms is our propensity to live in secrecy. What happens in the family stays in the family. We have been taught to not speak about "family business" outside of the family. Our parents ingrained this principle of secrecy in us at a very young age, and here's the thing… there is also a good chance that you have taught this same principle to your own child(ren). But, here is the problem with this principle: With so many African Americans being subjected to abuse, living in secrecy does not promote healing—it only serves to keep the abused broken and vulnerable. Abuse thrives in the darkness. Healing cannot begin until what is in the dark is exposed to the light. Therefore, while your child may have been sexually abused, because she was taught to keep a secret, she may not tell.

Another concern within the African American community is our tendency to protect family members at all cost. While we love our family and will do just about anything for them, we do not get to choose our family. The reality is that if we were allowed to pick our family, there are some kinfolks who would not have made it into the familial fold. As mentioned above, sexual abuse has occurred many times at the hands of a family member. So, instead of protecting the family at all cost, when your child tells you that Uncle so-and-so or Cousin so-and-so touched her, believe her. Regardless of who the perpetrator may be—family or not, we must stand up for our girls. We must believe our girls and not dismiss them. It is important that we listen when our daughters come to us with their concerns, because how we respond will determine what they will share in the future. Instead of protecting the family at all cost, let us protect our girls.

THERAPY AND THE AFRICAN AMERICAN COMMUNITY

It is no secret that the African American community does not embrace the idea of therapy. Since therapy is such a taboo subject within our community, perhaps it would be beneficial for us to talk about what therapy is and what it's not. Let's start by dispelling the myths and addressing some concerns.

THERAPY IS FOR CRAZY PEOPLE:

You may have grown up hearing folks say that therapy is for "crazy people", but as our society is beginning to embrace mental health and wellness, this myth is being dispelled. As a proud and resilient community, African Americans take pride in their ability to overcome any obstacle they face. However, this same pride prevents us from asking for help and seeking the support we desperately need. Therapy is not for "crazy people"; it is for people who desire to be healed and made whole.

YOU DON'T NEED THERAPY IF YOU HAVE FAITH:

Believers, Christians, Saints—however you may refer to those who are members of the Christian family—are often the most resistant to seeking therapy. Therapy and mental health are rarely spoken about in the Black Church, which can leave African American Christians confused about their walk with Christ and their need to address their mental health crisis. There is a myth we have embraced that says that if we have faith in God, then we don't need therapy. "Faith and only faith will get us through." But, while having faith is necessary for healing, the fact is, seeking the support of therapy is not a reflection of our lack of faith. God has made available to us all the tools and has equipped individuals with the education to help us in our healing process. It is important that we utilize all the resources that are available to us. Seek Christian Counseling if necessary, but never dismiss the power of faith combined with therapy. "Jesus and therapy go hand in hand." There is no shame in seeking therapy.

SO...WHAT IS THERAPY?

When we experience trauma such as sexual abuse, therapy is an effective tool in the healing process. Therapy is an appointed time with a licensed professional to help you navigate behaviors, thoughts, feelings, and much more.

Therapy can be one-on-one or in a group setting. Both group and individual therapy sessions are confidential. You may consider both individual and group therapy for the young lady you are concerned about. Group therapy can be an effective tool for your child, as they get the chance to interact with other children who have gone through similar experiences, and therefore do not feel alone.

It is important to note that one of the goals of therapy is to treat the client as well as the family. This is referred to as "treating the whole person." It is based on the belief that working with the immediate family yields a more effective outcome than working with the client alone. Therapy can be useful for other family members to learn how to support the victim through this difficult time.

Once you have decided to seek help for your daughter, then you will need to explain this to her. Allow her, if old enough, to be a part of the process of choosing a therapist. This includes a male or female therapist, individual therapy, and/or group counseling (support groups).

As a survivor of childhood sexual abuse, I entered therapy as an adult. Although I was and remain a believer in therapy, I initially did not think I needed it. I talked about my abuse with those whom I trusted. I believed everything in my life was going well, so it never occurred to me to seek counseling. I was sure I was fine and had overcome a horrific time in my life. It was not until those who were close to me noticed behaviors that were concerning and brought them to my attention. I recall having an honest conversation with a dear friend. On that day, my perspective changed. My friend presented me with thought-provoking questions that forced me to seek the answers through prayer, which then led me to therapy. There began my true journey to healing.

Therapy was challenging. I had to relive all the details of my abuse while processing those feelings I had (sub)consciously buried. As a part of my healing, I journaled about my feelings and wrote my story of abuse. My journal logs started out as thoughts but then formed into poetry. Journaling was therapeutic for me. Everything I wanted to say to my abuser, I wrote. Every fear, hurt, every angry thought I had, I wrote it down. When I finished pouring everything out, I had a collection of poetry, and I was able to see my growth in my writing. It was in therapy that I learned that the abuse was not my fault. Therapy taught me that I was worthy of love and deserving of receiving love. It was a painful, yet liberating experience for me. Some days, I left sessions in tears from the hurt I had to dig up, and other days, I was walking on water, proud and resilient.

The expression "Therapy works if you work it" speaks to the work that is required of the person attending therapy. People tend to shy away from therapy because it is hard work. It can be emotionally daunting and draining. Therapy requires a made-up mind—a determination. As a parental guardian, you must have a determined spirit to keep going even when your daughter wants to give up. While this is undoubtedly a difficult step for you and your family, it is a necessary one for healing to begin. Your daughter, niece, or granddaughter will need your love and support through this process.

CONTINUAL CARE

In seeking support, it is important to find a therapist who specializes in childhood sexual trauma. Life's difficult conversations can be made a little less difficult when we are talking to someone we trust. Also, note that therapy is most effective when it is continuous. It is not like taking a magic pill and things will change overnight. It will be challenging for that young lady and for your family. It will take time and a great amount of patience. So, prepare yourself for the journey. Tap into your support system and anticipate some difficult times. Be aware of setbacks and events that may trigger memories of the abuse. These are all expected on the healing journey and are normal. Share these concerns in therapy, but keep in mind that healing is a continuous process. Know that, in spite of the challenges, it will all be worth it.

WALKING INTO HEALING

CONCLUSION

Forgiveness and Boundaries

In spite of the abuse I have endured, I have learned to forgive. I have forgiven my cousin for what he has done. I want you to know that God is a Healer. He is the only One who could have healed me. I am grateful for the love of my parents, and the support of loved ones. I am grateful for therapy. I am grateful for all the tools and resources that aided me on my healing journey, but I am most grateful to God for the power to forgive.

There are some survivors who are not able to forgive their abusers. Others are not interested in forgiveness. And guess what? That's okay. It is important that we respect everyone's journey of healing. What one survivor may be able to do, another may not. It is not about comparison, it's about healing. While forgiveness is important to me, boundaries are just as important.

I had to establish healthy boundaries in my life, particularly regarding my abuser. This was a necessary measure as my abuser was a family member and there was a chance that I would see him during family events. I made the decision not to engage him in conversation and limit family events where he would be in attendance. Help your child to set healthy boundaries in their healing journey. This includes assessing safe spaces and appropriately responding when she shares her concerns about feeling safe.

FINAL THOUGHTS

I recently did an interview during which I spoke about life after abuse. I was able to recall something I had forgotten, or at least had not verbalized to anyone. I remembered the day that I decided I was going to tell my mother that I was being abused by my cousin. All day at school I walked around saying to myself, "Today is going to be the day." I decided that that day would be the day that I was going to be brave enough to tell my mom. I didn't know how I was going to do it, but I knew that that day had to be the day. I remembered when I made my way home, I still wasn't sure how I was going to share what had happened and honestly, I was still talking myself into sharing the secret that I kept to myself for some time. As mentioned earlier in the book, I eventually revealed it by writing my mother a note.

As I reflected on that day while doing the interview I smiled. I smiled because I thought about the brave step I took, and how I was believed and supported by my parents.

Let me reiterate—the fear of not being believed is one of the main reasons survivors remain silent. They remain silent as young girls and develop into women, still… silent. Silence and fear are the enemy. It prevents young girls from speaking their truth. The climate and culture of our society validate the need for support for survivors of sexual abuse. A part of that need is recognizing the signs and addressing sexual abuse.

It is crucial that we give our children a solid foundation and support them through every trial to help sustain them through life's challenges. My parents' discipline and my relationship with God were the foundation that I needed to help survive a traumatic time in my life. Your love and support will aid in your daughter, niece, or granddaughter's healing process. You are the lifeline that they need.

Abuse, as awful as it is, does not have to be the end. Life goes on, and healing is possible. Trauma can shape us in many ways. As a school and mental health counselor who works with children and adolescents, I was asked one day if I would have become a counselor if I'd never experienced abuse. I hesitated with my response, but after some thought, I realized that the abuse played a significant role in my career choices. While I'm sure you wish they didn't have to deal with the effects of abuse, believe me when I tell you that your daughter, your granddaughter, your niece—that princess—will be shaped by their trauma, but she will find her own path to healing, and she will be made whole. I did, and so will she.

References

- RAINN. (n.d.). *Children and Teens: Statistics*. https://www.rainn.org/statistics/children-and-teens

- The National Center on Violence against Women in the Black Community. (2018, October). *Statistics of Black Women and Sexual Assault* [Infographic]. https://ujimacommunity.org/wp-content/uploads/2018/12/Ujima-Womens-Violence-Stats-v7.4-1.pdf

Resources for Support

- Child Help: National Child Abuse Hotline - 1.800.422.4453

- The Mama Bear Effect: www.themamabeareffect.org

- Department of Human Services — Keep Kids Safe: www.keepkidssafe.pa.gov.